HEINEMANN
Profiles

Neil Armstrong

An Unauthorized Biography

Sean Connolly

Heinemann Library
Des Plaines, Illinois

Designed by Visual Image
Printed in Hong Kong / China

03 02 01 00 99

10 9 8 7 6 5 4 3 2 1

Library of Congress Cataloging-in-Publication Data
Connolly, Sean, 1956-
    Neil Armstrong / Sean Connolly.
      p. cm. -- (Heinemann profiles)
    Includes bibliographical references and index.
    Summary: Presents the childhood, career, and family life of the
first human being to set foot on the moon.
    ISBN 1-57572-692-0
    1. Armstrong, Neil, 1930- --Juvenile literature. 2. Astronauts-
-United States--Biography--Juvenile literature. [1. Armstrong,
Neil, 1930- . 2. Astronauts.] I. Title. II. Series.
TL789.85.A75C66 1998
629.45'0092--dc21
    [B]   98-7465
                                      CIP
                                        AC

Acknowledgments
The Publishers would like to thank the following for permission to reproduce photographs: AP p43 Aviation Picture Library p. 20; Austin J. Brown p. 11; Corbis/Bettman/UPI pp. 9, 21, 24, 28, 30, 31, 33, 41, 47, 48, 49; Popperfoto pp. 42, 44 (upper); Science Photo Library, p. 13, NASA pp. 30, 39, 44 (lower), 53; NASA/Science and Society Picture Library pp. 4, 32, 37, 40, 46; Smithsonian Institution pp7, 8, 12, 27; John Topham Picture Library p. 23.

Cover photograph reproduced with permission of The Hulton-Getty Picture Collection Ltd.
Every effort has been made to contact copyright holders of any material reproduced in this book. Any omissions will be rectified in subsequent printings if notice is given to the Publisher.

Any words appearing in the text in bold, **like this,** are explained in the Glossary.

This is an unauthorized biography. The subject has not sponsored or endorsed this book.

CONTENTS

WHO IS NEIL ARMSTRONG?

Neil Armstrong was the first human being to set foot on the moon. His historic achievement took place on July 20, 1969 and was watched by hundreds of millions of television viewers around the world. The task of sending an **astronaut** to the moon and back had been the goal of the United States since the early 1960s, and in 1961 President John F. Kennedy promised to make it happen before 1970.

TO THE MOON

Armstrong and fellow astronaut Buzz Aldrin beat that target by just over five months. Although proud

Armstrong's good nature and leadership qualities were ideal for the first lunar missions.

of their achievement, the two astronauts, particularly Armstrong, viewed the moon landing as a team effort. Armstrong would prefer to be considered an American hero, or even a representative of the whole planet, rather than an individual who looked for and achieved glory.

THE MAN BEHIND THE ACHIEVEMENT

At the time of the moon landing, Armstrong fitted many people's ideas of what an American hero should be. He was boyish looking, with a grin that would sometimes light up his whole face; he came from the farming heartland of the United States and was brought up to be hard working and obedient.

This picture, however, tells only part of the story: Armstrong is more complicated than such a simple image suggests. Few people would be able to cope with his hard training during the astronaut program and the efforts needed for the moon landing in particular. Armstrong's life in the decades since his famous moon walk also sheds light on his character. Removed from the bustling world of space launches and politics, he has found peace with his family back on a farm in Ohio.

What sort of person can sit back so happily after achieving something so incredible?

Neil Alden Armstrong was born on a farm in Wapakoneta, in Ohio, on August 5, 1930. His father, Stephen Armstrong, worked for the state of Ohio as an **auditor** and traveled throughout the state checking the finances of towns and cities. Because of this constant moving, Neil's mother Viola was eager to give birth to her first child in a familiar place. The farm where Neil was born belonged to Viola Armstrong's parents, the Korspeters.

Grandmother Korspeter's own parents had **emigrated** from Germany to the United States. They had worked hard to make their way from New York City to the rich farming country of Ohio. These lessons of determination and honest hard work were important to Grandmother Korspeter, and she passed them on to Neil, Neil's younger sister June, and brother Dean.

Difficult times

Neil was lucky to have such loving parents and grandparents, but he was also lucky to live in a family where there was a steady income. When Neil was born, the United States and much of the rest of the world had entered the **Great Depression**. Throughout most of the 1930's many people were **unemployed**, so the Armstrongs were fortunate, even though they had to move regularly.

AIRPORT EXCITEMENT

The air races of the early 1930's were exciting events in which pilots often risked their lives in flimsy airplanes.

The Armstrongs lived in Cleveland, Ohio's largest city, when Neil was very young. In those days, during the early 1930s, Cleveland was one of the few places in the state to have an airport. Most of the state was farming country. Neil's father loved airplanes and often took Neil to Cleveland's airport to watch the planes take off and land. Held in his father's arms, Neil would gaze in wonder at the aircraft.

The 1932 National Air Races attracted many excited spectators.

Neil's interest in flying developed further when he was only two years old, during another visit to the airport at Cleveland. The airport was organizing the National Air Races, and large crowds had come to watch the event. Neil had never seen anything travel so fast or so high, although now we would find the same aircraft slow and old-fashioned. There were even **biplanes** among the aircraft. They were slower than the planes with one wing, but they could perform thrilling **acrobatics** and even seemed to be able to stand still in the air.

On the Move

These experiences had a deep effect on the young Neil Armstrong. Looking back as an adult, he recalls how his interest in flying took off with these early visits to the Cleveland airport. Soon after these visits, though, the Armstrongs moved to Warren, Ohio, which was much smaller. Warren had no airport to compare with Cleveland's. Would the move mean the end of Neil's interest in flying?

Long lines of unemployed men seeking work were a common sight in the United States during the Depression.

Depression in the United States

The Great Depression was a time when many people struggled to find work to support their families. It began with the New York stock market crash of 1929 and continued until 1939, when the **Second World War** began. Banks had to close and as many as 12 million Americans were **unemployed**. Many farmers lost their farms because prices for crops were too low to help pay off the farmers' debts.

The Desire for Flying

Neil was an intelligent and curious little boy, and his questions were not just about **aviation**. He and his family would listen to the news on the radio, and Neil would ask his parents questions about what he had just heard. His mother would answer his questions patiently, even when Neil wanted to know more and more about a subject.

Exploring through books

This curiosity also showed in Neil's schoolwork. He learned to read quickly, and his report cards showed top grades in all subjects. Reading, however, was Neil's real introduction to the world around him. During his first year in school, he read a book about the Wright brothers, who developed the first airplane in 1903. Orville and Wilbur Wright had worked on that first aircraft in their workshop in Dayton, Ohio, which was not far from the farm where Neil's grandparents lived.

Into the air

One Sunday morning in July 1936, Neil's father came into the kitchen with some news. An interesting plane was coming into the airport that morning. He went on to tell the family that this was a very big plane, a Ford Tri-Motor, and it was made of metal. It was nicknamed the "Tin Goose" because it looked like a huge flying goose and because

The Ford Tri-Motor got its name from its three engines, one at its nose and one on each wing. people thought that it was made from tin, although it was really made from aluminium.

The plane was due to take off at noon, when the Armstrongs would still be at church. Neil's mother suggested that Neil and his father go for a quick look before church. As Neil was looking at the **propellers** of the three engines, one of the pilots offered to take the father and son up for a ride. Neil was overjoyed as the plane raced down the runway and took off. He watched as the buildings and people grew smaller and was thrilled as the plane dipped its wing and turned during the flight. He was still excited as the plane touched down once more on the runway.

Building detailed models of airplanes strengthened Neil's love of flying.

MODEL FOR THE FUTURE

Later in the summer, after Neil's flight in the "Tin Goose," he and his mother passed a hobby shop in town. Neil persuaded his mother to buy him a model plane kit. He patiently assembled the balsa wood pieces and proudly placed the completed model on the shelf by his bed.

Neil began to make other models from the light balsa wood, hoping that he could build one that would fly. He completed one of the models while the family was staying at his grandparents' farm. Daylight was fading by the time he took the completed model outside. While his

parents and grandparents watched from the porch, Neil wound up the elastic band of the model's **propeller** and gave the plane a toss. It caught a breeze and soared into the summer air before coming back to the ground safely.

The light weight of the Wright brother's first airplane helped it catch the breezes on the North Carolina beach.

The Wright brothers

The Wright brothers, Wilbur (1867–1912) and Orville (1871–1948), invented the first successful airplane. They were trained as bicycle mechanics and used their Ohio workshop to experiment with different types of wings and propellers. Their first flight, with Orville as pilot, took place at Kitty Hawk, North Carolina, on December 17, 1903. The flight lasted only a few seconds but it opened the door to air and space travel.

Into the Air

The Armstrong family remained on the move as Mr. Armstrong continued his job as state auditor. Neil did well at each new school, and his excellent reading let him skip the second year of school so that he joined a class where everyone was a year older than he was. During these early years at school, Neil began collecting magazines about flying and kept a scrapbook in which he pasted pictures of aircraft.

New friends

Neil was eleven years old when his family moved to Upper Sandusky, Ohio. In his new school, Neil made many new friends. Two of his best friends were Konstantin Solacoff and Bud Blackford. They shared Neil's interest in building model planes, and the three friends would fly them together, sometimes from Neil's bedroom window upstairs in the Armstrong's house.

As a boy, Neil Armstrong eagerly learned about aviation by building wooden models of airplanes.

Around this time, Neil got his first job, helping the caretaker of the local cemetery to mow the lawns on Saturdays or after school. Neil earned ten cents an hour and saved the money to buy more flying magazines.

THE EFFECTS OF WAR

The **Second World War** had been going on in Europe for more than two years when the United States entered the conflict on December 7, 1941. The people in Upper Sandusky, like other Americans, had to help with the **war effort**. Meat and other foods, as well as gasoline, were **rationed**, which meant that Neil visited his grandparents less often. Balsa wood was also rationed because it was used to build fighter planes, so Neil had to use wood scraps, straw, and paper to build his models, which he also designed.

As a way of building community spirit, a Boy Scout troop was organized for the first time in Upper Sandusky. Neil's father was the assistant scoutmaster and several friends joined Neil in Troop 25.

THE TRAINEE PILOT

Neil was still a Boy Scout in 1944 when his family moved for the last time, this time back to Wapakoneta, near his grandparents. Mr. Armstrong was the scoutmaster in the Wapakoneta troop, and he was pleased when Neil and some of his fellow scouts began studying for their **astronomy** badge. The scout patrol visited a small local **observatory** and got to know Jacob Zint, the man who built it. Neil had decided to become a pilot and an **aeronautical engineer**, and he knew that a knowledge of the skies was vital.

With these same ambitions in mind, Neil began to spend a great deal of time at Port Koneta Airport a few miles outside the town. There he washed planes to earn pocket money to add to the 40 cents an hour he earned at a local pharmacy. His plan was to

Washing planes earned Armstrong pocket money and it also helped him learn more about aircraft design.

Armstrong learned to fly in a single engine Aeronca Champion. save up for flying lessons, which cost nine dollars an hour. Neil's parents agreed to this plan, and he took his first flying lesson at the age of 15.

Neil got his student pilot's license on August 5, 1946, his sixteenth birthday. He was on his way to becoming a pilot—would he be as successful in his plans to become an aeronautical engineer?

All that jazz

School assemblies at Wapakoneta often had musical performances from some of the students. Neil and some of his friends decided to set up a small jazz band for these performances. Neil played baritone horn, Jerre Maxson and Bob Gustafson played trombone, and Jim Mouget played clarinet. The quartet called themselves the Mississippi Moonshiners. Neil's musical ability would later let him entertain and amuse fellow pilots and **astronauts**.

A Boost from the Navy

Neil was very happy to be back in Wapakoneta. Not only was the family once more living near his grandparents' farm, but he was doing particularly well in his school, Blume High School. His model making had become so advanced that he tested his planes in a home-made **wind tunnel**. At a parents and teachers evening, Neil's science teacher told Mr. and Mrs. Armstrong that their son should continue his studies and go to college. This news made the Armstrongs proud, but a university was very expensive. How could they possibly afford it?

A Navy Scholarship

In Neil's last year at high school, he received a **scholarship** from the U.S. Navy, which would pay his way through the university of his choice. He had almost forgotten that he had written to them but was very excited when a letter arrived. He ran to the basement door to call down to his mother, who was

Armstrong's scholarship meant that he could go to college as long as he served in the Navy afterwards.

gathering some jars of fruit. Startled by the shouting, Mrs. Armstrong dropped a jar on her foot and broke her toe. But the pain was nothing compared to the pride she felt in her son's achievement.

FIRST TASTE OF COLLEGE

Neil chose to attend Purdue University in Indiana, the state next to Ohio. It had a good **aeronautical engineering** program and it was not very far from home. He enjoyed learning in the new place among people who shared his interests.

Halfway through the second year of Neil's four-year course, there was a shock. The United States looked ready to enter another conflict, this time helping the **United Nations** in the Asian country of South Korea. Neil, with his Navy scholarship, knew that his days at the university were numbered.

Old friends

Neil Armstrong also enjoyed the social side of his new life at college. Not long after starting at Purdue, he joined a band to play baritone horn. To his surprise and great pleasure, he found that his friend Bud Blackford from Upper Sandusky was also in the band. The two friends remained close throughout their college days.

ACTIVE DUTY

Neil Armstrong was only 19 years old when the U.S. Navy called him into **active duty**. He was sent to a naval air base in Pensacola, Florida, for flight training. This involved learning how to fly the latest fighter planes, and Neil chose to train on single-engine jet fighters. These planes are fast, but they are also involved in some of the most dangerous fighting missions.

Armstrong became a fighter pilot soon after the Korean War broke out on June 25, 1950. He was part of the first all-jet fighter **squadrons** to be sent into action. Armstrong and the other squadron members were based on the USS *Essex*, an **aircraft carrier** that sailed in the Pacific Ocean near Korea.

BATTLE EXPERIENCE

Armstrong's fighter squadron had been trained for air-to-air combat: pilots were expected to attack enemy aircraft and shoot them down in **dogfights**. However, there were no enemy fighters in the area, so the squadron became involved in different.

Panthers, like the one Armstrong flew in Korea, were among the world's first jet fighters.

missions. They had to fly low into enemy territory and then damage bridges, factories, and other targets.

These flying missions were very dangerous and required both bravery and flying skills. On one mission, Armstrong was flying through a valley when a cable clipped off part of one wing of his fighter plane. The cable had been put there as a **booby trap**. Armstrong got his damaged plane back over safe territory before parachuting down. On another mission, he managed to fly a damaged fighter plane back to the USS *Essex* and land it safely.

EXPERIENCE FOR THE FUTURE

Many members of Armstrong's fighter squadron were killed or wounded. Low flying through heavy **anti-aircraft** fire was the major risk.

Landing a plane on the deck of the aircraft carrier was also very dangerous if the sea was heavy and the deck was rolling. The practical experience of these wartime conditions would be valuable for Armstrong in his later life.

Armstrong's Korean War duty ended in the middle of 1952. He had flown 78 combat missions and had received three air medals for his outstanding service and bravery.

A SAFE RETURN

Neil Armstrong had good reason to feel pleased with his career so far. Although he was only 22 years old, he had fulfilled one of his aims, to become a pilot, and gone on to help his country. He had gained valuable flying experience in nearly every type of flying condition and had flown some of the world's most advanced aircraft.

But becoming a pilot had been only part of Armstrong's ambition. He still wanted to become an **aeronautical engineer** and he was eager to complete his college education. In the fall of 1952, after his Korean missions were completed, Neil Armstrong returned to Purdue University. He could look forward to hard bookwork and studying and felt that his days of danger and high excitement were over. Or were they?

The Korean War

The Korean War lasted from 1950 to 1953. It began when North Korea, a **communist** country, attacked South Korea, which supported **western** ideals. This period began a tense time known as the **Cold War**, and the **United Nations** tried to stop the conflict from spreading beyond Korea. U.S. armed forces supported the South Korean army, while North Korea received troops and aid from communist China. After three years of fighting, which claimed the lives of nearly three million people, a **cease-fire** was declared and the fighting stopped.

Airborne fighting played a large part in the Korean War on land and at sea.

Back to the Books

Armstrong went back to Purdue University for the school year beginning in the fall of 1952. Because of his two years spent in the Navy, he was slightly older than some of his classmates; the wartime experience had also made him more mature. His goal was the degree in **aeronautical engineering**.

New interests

The hard work and maturity did not stop Armstrong from joining in many new activities and making new friends. He became a member of the Institute of Aeronautical Sciences and the American Rocket Society, and he was president of the Aero Club, which concentrated on flying.

One of his new friends was a dark-haired girl named Jan Shearon. She was a fellow student who came from Chicago and shared many of Neil's interests, especially flying and music. They began seeing more of each other and started dating when Neil had graduated from Purdue in January 1955.

DREAMING OF SPACE

Armstrong hoped to get a job at Edwards Air Force Base in California, where the National Advisory Committee on Aeronautics (NACA, which later became the National Aeronautics and Space Administration, or **NASA**) was doing some interesting tests. There were no jobs at Edwards, but Armstrong was offered a job at the Lewis Flight Propulsion Laboratory in Cleveland, Ohio. There he learned more about rocket technology and got many chances to fly.

Not long after beginning at Lewis, though, Armstrong got a call from Edwards Air Force Base. There was now a job there and it was his for the taking. Armstrong said yes and got warm support from the colleagues he was leaving at the Lewis Laboratory. Armstrong's personal space age was about to begin.

Start of the Space Age

Scientists had long believed that rockets could eventually launch **satellites** into outer space, beyond the earth's **atmosphere**. That belief became reality in October 1957, when the Soviet Union launched Sputnik, the first satellite to circle the earth outside the atmosphere. U.S. scientists were impressed but also worried that satellites could be used for military purposes. Much more research and money were poured into efforts to match the Soviet achievement.

TEST PILOT

A rmstrong was enthusiastic as he set off on the 2,200 mile (3,540 kilometer) drive from Ohio to California. His thoughts were on the exciting flying advances being made under the desert sky, where high-**altitude** flights were going to the outer edges of the earth's **atmosphere**.

But just as he set off west on his way to California, Armstrong turned north to Wisconsin, where Jan Shearon was working at a summer camp. He asked her to marry him and to go to California. She agreed, and they were married in the following winter of 1956.

Armstrong's growing family—shown here in 1969—gave him a supportive base while he was a test pilot and astronaut.

At Edwards Air Force Base, Neil Armstrong joined the team of brave and daring test pilots.

Life at Edwards

Most of the people who worked at Edwards Air Force Base lived in the nearby town of Lancaster, California. But the newly married couple loved the countryside near the base and chose to live in a former forest ranger's cabin high up in the San Gabriel Mountains. Their first child, Eric, was born a year after they arrived, and their daughter, Karen, was born in 1959.

Armstrong arrived at Edwards Air Force Base and began his new career as a **test pilot**. This dangerous job involved flying **prototypes** of new aircraft and testing the limits of their ability. Sometimes a flight would test how high an aircraft could fly; other flights would test the speed or turning ability of an airplane.

Help for the "Space Race"

By 1960 **NASA** was planning to send an **astronaut** into space. This was the period of the **Cold War** and the U.S. government knew that the **Soviet Union** had similar plans. Both governments believed that it was important to lead in this **space race** because they felt that the space programs were symbols of their importance as nations. NACA had changed its name to NASA to reflect the new importance of space.

The sleek X-15 aircraft looked more like a rocket than an airplane.

The NASA program trained **astronauts** to fly alone in a *Mercury* space capsule. The capsule would be launched from a huge rocket and sent into space, but it would also be traveling very fast when it returned to earth. The research teams at Edwards Air Force Base tested the parachutes that the capsule would use. Armstrong and other **test pilots** took a full-sized model of the space capsule to an altitude of 23,333 yards (21,336 meters). They tried different types of parachutes in a series of test drops until they found one that was strong enough and not too bulky.

NEW HEIGHTS

Armstrong continued his test flights in some of the most advanced aircraft. He was one of only a handful

Watching the launch

The X–15 aircraft did not take off from the ground like normal airplanes. Instead it was launched from the air, dropping from a Boeing B–52 airship. From her cabin high up in the mountains, Jan Armstrong watched with binoculars as Neil's X–15 left the B–52 and sped into the sky. Later, she could see the dust cloud form in the valley as the X–15 landed on the 25 miles (40 kilometer) dry lake bed at Edwards Air Force Base.

of pilots to fly the X–15, a sleek, winged rocket plane that would drop from another plane, shoot off to the edge of the atmosphere, and then glide back to earth without power. The X–15 could reach altitudes of over 200,000 feet (60,960 meters), almost six times higher than the height at which a modern jumbo jet travels.

Armstrong's sixth X–15 flight in 1962 took him to a height of 207, 500 feet (63,094 meters.) The steady climb from earth leveled off there, and the plane was suspended for a few moments. From the **cockpit,** Armstrong could see the bright horizon of the earth curving below a black sky. This was close to space travel, but would he ever have the chance to take the next step and venture into the blackness?

We were using airplanes as tools to gather all kinds of information, just as an **astronomer** uses a telescope as a tool. We didn't fly often, but when we did, it was unbelievably exciting.

Neil Armstrong, looking back at his years at Edwards Air Force Base

The Sky's the Limit

Armstrong's **aeronautical engineering** background had made him one of the most valuable **test pilots** at Edwards Air Force Base. Armstrong enjoyed the flight research as much as the flying itself. But that glimpse of the inky darkness had made Armstrong hungry for space travel. What is more, his next test project, flying the newly-designed Dyno-Soar glider even higher, might be canceled as NASA concentrated on its astronaut program.

One of "The Nine"

On September 17, 1962, Neil Armstrong was accepted as a **NASA astronaut.** He was the first astronaut who was a **civilian** and joined the second group of astronauts who were known as "the nine."

Soon after joining NASA in 1962 Armstrong (front row, second from right) posed with other astronauts by models of the Mercury, Gemini, and Apollo spacecraft.

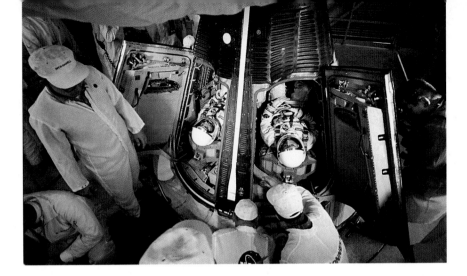

Close teamwork between astronauts and engineers was needed to produce a workable space capsule.

The first group, "The Seven," were involved with the one-man **Mercury** missions. The Mercury missions were important, but they were seen as a first stage in the goal of eventually landing an astronaut on the moon.

NASA's TARGET

Armstrong and the other astronauts were aware of the pressures they faced. Only a year before Armstrong had become an astronaut, President John F. Kennedy had promised the world that the United States would land an astronaut on the moon before 1970. That date was less than eight years away, and the Mercury missions had simply **orbited** the Earth and returned. So much needed to be learned before a spacecraft could travel 240,000 miles (386,160 kilometers) to the moon and then return.

> I believe this nation should commit itself, before the decade is out, to landing a man on the Moon and returning him safely to the Earth.
>
> President John F. Kennedy, May 1961

What sort of risks did the astronauts face along the way?

THE GEMINI YEARS

The *Gemini* space capsule sat at the top of a powerful Titan 2 rocket, which powered it into orbit.

Armstrong and the other members of "the nine" trained for missions in the two-person *Gemini* space capsules. These capsules would **orbit** the earth longer than those in the *Mercury* program and would help prepare for the eventual **lunar** flights. Training was long and hard, and **NASA** officials tried to re-create the experience of space flight on special training grounds.

Sometimes the **astronauts** would be spun at incredible speeds on a **centrifuge** to get used to the high speeds of the spacecraft. They would sit in a model of the *Gemini* **cockpit** and have to carry out the jobs they would do on a real flight. Other tests took them into high-flying planes where they would experience short periods of **weightlessness**. Life at home was also very busy as the Armstrongs' youngest child, Mark, was born in 1963.

THE FIRST TEST

Each Gemini space flight had certain aims. Some had to practice **docking** with other objects in space because the real lunar mission would

rely on such moves. Other flights concentrated on staying in **orbit** for as long as possible to test the astronauts' endurance. The pilot and copilot of each mission would practice the specific routines for months in advance, but so did their **backup crew**, who had to be ready to replace them in case there was an accident or if someone became ill.

Armstrong was in the backup for *Gemini 5*, which was due for takeoff in August 1965.

Armstrong remained on Earth as **astronauts** Gordon Cooper and Pete Conrad orbited for eight days, a record for U.S. astronauts. Armstrong's preparations, however, had put him in a good position to fly in a later mission. His chance was to come in less than seven months, on board *Gemini 8*.

EMERGENCY!

On March 16, 1966 Neil Armstrong and his co-pilot David Scott took off on *Gemini 8*. The goal of the mission was to dock with an unoccupied (nobody driving it) orbiting satellite, the *Agena*. The astronauts would have to position their *Gemini* spacecraft in order to meet the **satellite** and then join the two together in space.

Armstrong and Scott adjusted the **thrusters** of the *Gemini* to join the **orbit** of the *Agena* and then close in on it. The docking worked perfectly, but when the two astronauts examined their instruments, the joined spacecraft began to tumble faster and faster. If it continued, Armstrong knew, the tumbling could

Flying the college flag

Few people were prouder of Neil Armstrong than the teachers and students of Purdue University, which he had attended about ten years before his flight. Armstrong had even carried a black and gold Purdue flag with him on the flight. He presented it to the president of Purdue when he was honored there in May 1966.

Armstrong and Scott prepare for the last stage of the countdown for their Gemini 8 mission.

break the two craft apart. He undocked, but the *Gemini* capsule began to spin even faster, spinning a full turn every second. The sun and the earth kept flashing through their window.

Armstrong realized that one of the thrusters had stuck open. He had to think quickly and used the **reentry** thrusters to steady the spacecraft. Using these backup thrusters meant calling a halt to the mission, and *Gemini 8* returned to earth safely after only ten hours.

A GOOD OMEN

NASA officials were grateful that Armstrong's quick thinking and steady nerves had saved the spacecraft, not to mention the lives of all the crew members. Armstrong's bravery on *Gemini 8* made an impression on those people who were thinking of who would travel on the **lunar** mission.

Preparing for the Moon

Despite the problems, including the **thruster** incident on Armstrong's *Gemini 8* mission, **NASA** believed that the space program was ready to enter its next stage. From now on, the missions would use *Apollo* spacecraft, the type they planned to send to the moon.

The strategy

The *Apollo* spacecraft would hold three **astronauts**. The first missions would practice even longer flights, docking with other spacecraft, and eventually flying to the moon without landing. In the eventual **lunar** mission, the spacecraft would travel to the moon where it would stay in **orbit**. Then two of the astronauts would go through a hatch to the **lunar module**, which would leave the orbiting spacecraft and go down to the moon's surface. After spending some time on the moon, the two astronauts would launch the lunar module and **dock** it once more with the orbiting spacecraft in order to return to earth.

Another crisis

Armstrong was part of the team that trained for these Apollo missions. Some of the most difficult training involved flying the Lunar Landing Research Vehicle (LLRV). The LLRV was a jet aircraft without wings, and was nicknamed the "flying bedstead" because of its awkward shape. Astronauts had to practice landing the LLRV to prepare for landing the lunar module on a real moon flight.

On May 6, 1968 Armstrong was landing the LLRV, and only 67 yards (61 meters) above the ground, smoke began to pour from the engine, and the LLRV began spinning. Then it rolled over and began tumbling toward the ground. After trying to correct the craft's movements, Armstrong hit the **ejection** switch and parachuted to safety while the LLRV crashed onto the runway and burst into flames.

NASA engineers spent thousands of hours developing the lunar module.

Scientists eventually discovered a problem in the design of the LLRV, and they agreed that it was only Armstrong's quick thinking, yet again, that had saved his life.

A TRAGIC SETBACK

Armstrong's near miss was dangerous, but because it had taken place on a training ground, the general public never heard about it. Instead, the news in the late 1960s was full of each new Apollo mission and the ever-nearer goal of landing on the moon. The news was mixed, however, and the first mission, *Apollo 1,* ended in tragedy before it even took off. The three **astronauts** died on the **launch pad**.

The later Apollo missions rekindled public enthusiasm for the space project again. By Christmas 1968, only seven months after Armstrong's LLRV crisis, *Apollo 8* became the first spacecraft to fly to the moon and back. The human-occupied landing seemed near at hand, but who would be the crew of this dramatic voyage?

THE NEWS BREAKS

NASA believed that the best crew for the **lunar** landing would be the team of astronauts who had practiced the most for a lunar flight. They decided that the **backup crew** for the successful *Apollo 8* mission would be the best choice. On January 9, 1969, the names of the crew for *Apollo 11,* the human–occupied landing, were announced to the public. They included two experienced astronauts, Edwin "Buzz" Aldrin and Michael Collins. The third member of the crew (and its captain) was Neil Armstrong.

The Apollo 11 crew: (from left) Neil Armstrong, Michael Collins, and "Buzz" Aldrin

Fire on *Apollo 1*

The first human-occupied Apollo mission was set to take off in February 1967. The crew was made up of veteran astronauts Gus Grisson and Ed White, along with newcomer Roger Chaffee. On January 27 the crew entered the *Apollo* capsule, which was in position at the top of a Saturn rocket, for a *simulated* countdown. About four hours into the practice, a fire broke out inside the capsule. It was so hot that neither the astronauts nor the ground crew could open the hatch door. All three astronauts died within seconds. The whole space program then seemed at risk.

THE MOON IN SIGHT

Everything was going ahead for the *Apollo 11* launch, which was scheduled for July 16, 1969. Michael Collins would **orbit** the moon in the **command module,** while Neil Armstrong and Buzz Aldrin would take the **lunar module** down to the moon's surface. But which of these two **astronauts** would be the first to set foot on the moon?

SPARED A TOUGH DECISION

Buzz Aldrin, like every other astronaut, would have liked to do it, but he knew that the decision was not his to make. Luckily for Armstrong, who did not want to appear greedy, the decision was not his either. One day in the spring of 1969, Deke Slayton, **NASA**'s Director of Flight Crew Personnel, met Armstrong and said that the plan was for Armstrong to go out first. He asked if Armstrong agreed. Armstrong replied, "Yes. That's the way to do it."

Armstrong and Aldrin had to become skilled with the tools they would use on the surface of the moon.

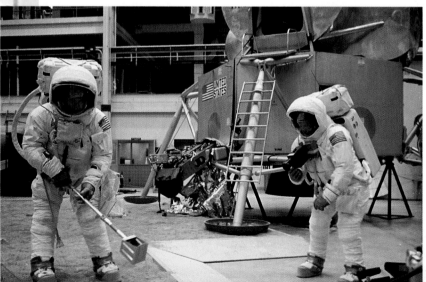

STILL MORE TRAINING

The crew of *Apollo 11* underwent more training than they had ever experienced. At the NASA Center at Langley, Virginia, there were full-scale replicas of the command module and the lunar module. The astronauts had to **simulate** flying them and to think of the problems that they might face, as well as how they would solve these difficulties.

Knowing the risks involved, and also aware of the tragic accidents that had happened along the way, NASA also invented more problems for the crew. During the spring and early summer of 1969, each of the three astronauts spent more than 400 hours working in the simulators.

With just two days to go before their historic Moon mission, Armstrong, Aldrin, and Collins still seemed relaxed at this July 14 press conference.

Meeting the press

On July 14, 1969, they faced members of the world's press and answered many questions about the mission they were about to undertake.

One reporter told Armstrong that, as the first person to set foot on the moon, his personal life would cease to exist. He meant that reporters would be always asking Armstrong and his family about the moon flight, and it would be hard to go anywhere without being recognized. Armstrong smiled: "I suppose if there is any recognizable disadvantage to being in the position I'm in then that's it. I think it's a fair trade."

ONE SMALL STEP

A s well as the hard training before the flight, there were other decisions to be made. The crew decided on the names of the **command module** and the **lunar module.** They would call the **command module** the *Columbia* in honor of an American song. The lunar module would be the *Eagle*, the symbol of the United States. Everything now seem ready for the incredible mission.

TAKE OFF

One million people had arrived at the Cape Kennedy launch site in Florida by the morning of July 16, 1969, the date of the *Apollo 11* launch. Another estimated 200 million watched on their televisions. Stephen and Viola Armstrong peered at their television set at their home in Wapakoneta, Ohio. With them was Viola's mother, the 81-year-old Grandmother Korspeter. The *Apollo 11* spacecraft

A million eager spectators saw the bright flash and heard the thunderous roar as Apollo 11 took off for the moon.

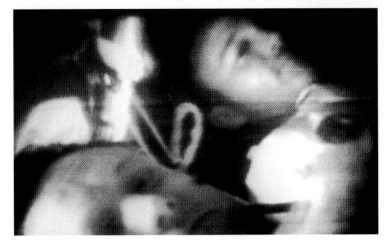

Television images of the *Apollo 11* astronauts kept the world informed of their progress to the moon.

looked tiny at the top of the huge Saturn 5 rocket, which would blast it out of the earth's **orbit**.

At exactly 9:32 a.m., *Apollo 11* blasted off and the surrounding area was shattered with the deafening sound of the rocket engines. From **mission control,** the last words were "Good luck and Godspeed." Armstrong replied "Thank you very much. We know this will be a good flight."

ON THE WAY

The Saturn rocket powered the *Apollo* spacecraft into orbit around the earth, and then more rockets increased its speed so that it could break free of the earth's **gravity** and continue on its flight to the moon. By this time, it was traveling at 24,200 miles (38,940 kilometers) per hour.

Halfway through the flight, the crew broadcast television pictures of life inside the spacecraft. Viewers watched Armstrong and Aldrin practice sliding through the narrow tunnel into the **lunar module**.

Neil Armstrong, who took the picture, is reflected in "Buzz" Aldrin's visor.

The crew also stayed in constant radio contact with **NASA** mission control in Houston, Texas. This is the home of the Manned Spacecraft Center and the headquarters for flight planning and communications. By the fourth day of their voyage, they were orbiting the moon.

THE *EAGLE* HAS LANDED

Armstrong and Aldrin slid into the lunar module, the *Eagle*, and began their descent to the moon just after 3:00 P.M. (Houston time) on July 20. Their planning had prepared them for this stage, but Armstrong noticed that their landing site, which was only the size of a soccer field, had many large rocks. He had to fly the *Eagle* to the surface himself

Armstrong and Aldrin plant the U.S. flag on the Moon on July 20, 1969.

Neil Armstrong: Houston. Tranquillity Base here. The *Eagle* has landed.

Mission Control: Roger, Tranquillity. We copy you on the ground. You got a lot of guys about to turn blue. We're breathing again. Thanks a lot.

July 20, 1969, 3:17 P.M.

without relying on the computer controls. At 3:17 P.M. they reached the moon's surface, the landing was so soft that neither **astronaut** noticed the impact. The landing site seemed to have lived up to its name of Tranquillity Base.

The famous words

It seems strange now, but the *Apollo 11* flight plan called for Armstrong and Aldrin to sleep for four hours before they got out of the *Eagle*. They felt so excited, however, that they asked to go out early. They slowly got into their heavy spacesuits, looking like Medieval knights putting on heavy suits of armor. By 9:28 P.M. (Houston time) they were able to open the hatch of the *Eagle* and descend the ladder to the moon.

Here men from the planet earth first set foot on the moon, July 1969. We came in peace for all mankind.

Inscription on a plaque left at the *Apollo 11* landing site

Aldrin pulled a ring inside the *Eagle,* and a television camera emerged to film the astronauts setting foot on the moon. Armstrong carefully put one boot on the **lunar** surface and said, "That's one small step for man, one giant leap for mankind."

45

World Acclaim

A rmstrong and Aldrin collected **lunar** rock samples, set up some scientific instruments to gather data, and planted an American flag in the lunar soil. They piloted the **lunar module** back to the *Columbia*. The *Apollo* spacecraft returned to earth on July 24, 1969, landing in the Pacific Ocean about 800 miles (1,287 kilometers) southwest of Hawaii. The **astronauts** waited in the floating capsule, until a Navy helicopter arrived. It lowered a strong cable to the capsule and the astronauts were hauled up in turn through a hatch to the helicopter, which then flew to the waiting aircraft carrier, USS *Hornet*.

A heroic welcome

Once on board the USS *Hornet* the crew of the *Apollo 11* were put in a quarantine trailer until **NASA** scientists were sure that they had not brought back any dangerous germs from the moon. U.S. President Richard Nixon flew to the *Hornet* and addressed the crew through a microphone.

U.S. President Richard Nixon welcomes the three lunar voyagers back to earth, saying, "This is the greatest week in the history of the world since the Creation."

UNITED STAT

46

HORNET + 3

Armstrong,
Aldrin, and
Collins received
hero's welcome as
their open-top
car paraded
through New
York City.

ONE BIG PARADE

The astronauts were flown to Houston and stayed in quarantine until August 10. Then they were honored in parades in New York City and Chicago and flown to Los Angeles for a state dinner with the president. There they received the nation's highest **civilian** honor, the Presidential Medal of Freedom.

Armstrong next visited his home town, Wapakoneta, Ohio. Thousands lined a parade route to cheer him. On September 16, the astronauts gave a speech to a **joint session** of the U.S. Congress.

Our successes in space lead us to hope that this strength can be used in the next decade in the solution of many of our planet's problems.
Neil Armstrong, addressing the U.S. Congress, September 16, 1969

Then came for a world tour. The cheering, tearful faces the astronauts saw showed that the lunar mission had not simply benefited the astronauts, or even the United States. Instead, they showed how the mission's aims, and success, stemmed from the human spirit itself.

Closing a Chapter

Neil Armstrong stayed with **NASA** after the news of the *Apollo 11* flight faded. He wanted to continue flying, but NASA chose him to run their aeronautics activities. The new job involved moving to Washington D.C., where Armstrong had never felt comfortable. He left that job after a year because he wanted to try another goal that he had kept quiet from some of his fellow **astronauts:** to teach.

Back to Ohio

In 1962 Armstrong had told some of his closest friends that he wanted to write an engineering textbook one day. He saw the chance when he was offered the job of professor of aerospace engineering at the University of Cincinnati, in his home state of Ohio. In 1971 Neil and Jan, along with their children, left the frantic world of Washington behind and bought a dairy farm near the city of Lebanon, Ohio. Armstrong stayed at the University of Cincinnati until 1979.

Keeping the net wide

Since leaving his teaching job, Armstrong has been involved in a number of businesses. He is chairperson

Away from the excitement of NASA, Armstrong gravitated to one of his other loves, engineering.

Armstrong addressed the U.S. Congress in September 1969. He later spent a year as a roving NASA ambassador, although he was never happy being in the public spotlight.

of the board of AIL Systems, an electronics company in New York, but he remains firmly based at his Ohio farm. Although he does not like being in the public eye, Armstrong has remained available for interviews and to help his former colleagues at NASA. In 1986, for example, he acted as vice-chairman of a team that investigated the *Challenger* space shuttle disaster, when seven astronauts lost their lives.

He died Aug. 25, 2012   82 years old   Complications following surgery to relieve blocked coronary arteries

This balance of a private life linked with public service has been Armstrong's strength throughout his career.

> You understand that you're a short-term phenomenon, like the mosquitoes that come in the spring and the fall. You get a perspective on yourself. You're getting back to the fundamentals of the planet. Neil feels that way, because we've talked about it, and so do I.
>
> Armstrong's friend Robert Holz,
> on Neil Armstrong's return to farming

ARMSTRONG THE MAN

Compared with some former **astronauts**, who appear regularly on television and give speeches, Neil Armstrong is a private person. Michael Collins, who flew with Armstrong on *Apollo 11,* was impressed by his intelligence but felt that he could never get to know the man. This view is echoed by people who have met Armstrong throughout his life: he is an intelligent, hard-working man but hard to understand.

THE LIGHTER SIDE

But it would be wrong to think of Neil Armstrong as always hard working and serious. The **test pilots** and astronauts who got to know him all agree that a certain shyness kept Armstrong from the limelight. They also agree on his ability to enjoy himself and on his mischievous sense of humor.

Rise and shine

While doing some difficult training as **backup crew** for *Gemini 11,* Armstrong pretended to be asleep as his copilot Bill Anders frantically tried to read a series of instruments. Armstrong "woke up" just in time to flip the right switch before winking at Anders.

The right man for the job

The scientists at **mission control** could not have asked for a better captain for the first **lunar** mission. Armstrong had long been admired for his intelligence, but when it was time to describe the sights on the moon, he startled **geologists** with the depth of his knowledge and his powers of observation.

As a test pilot in the 1950's Armstrong was a popular performer at the bar when the flying was over for the day. His lively jazz piano playing kept many parties going until late at night. And when rival pilots came into the room and made some requests for songs, Armstrong got his own group laughing at the expense of these newcomers. Years later he would play jokes on startled fellow astronauts.

Armstrong is shown in the Apollo spacesuit.

A TEAM PLAYER

Although some **NASA** officials wish Armstrong would appear publicly more often, most space officials believe that Armstrong's proud sense of privacy strengthens his role as a modest hero. After all, Armstrong has always been puzzled by the publicity that he still gets from his moon landing. For him it was always a team effort, and everyone should have felt proud on that memorable day in July 1969.

The lunar module took Armstrong to the surface of the moon.

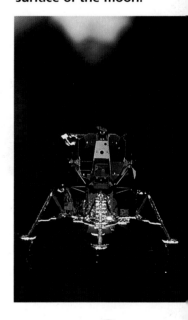

NEIL ARMSTRONG— TIMELINE

1930	Neil Alden Armstrong born on August 5 to Stephen and Viola Armstrong in Wapakoneta, Ohio
1932	Armstrong taken to Cleveland Airport to watch the airplanes
1936	Armstrong's first flight, in a Ford Tri-Motor ("Tin Goose")
1941	Family moves to Upper Sandusky, Ohio, where Neil Armstrong gets his first job (mowing lawns at local cemetery)
1942	Armstrong becomes a Boy Scout, and his father is assistant scoutmaster
1944	Family moves back to Wapakoneta
1945	Armstrong pays for his first flying lessons at Port Koneta Airport
1946	Receives student pilot's license
1947	Graduates from Blume High School and receives U.S. Navy **scholarship.** Enrolls at Purdue University, Indiana
1950	Called into active duty by U.S. Navy
1950–2	Involved in Korean War and flies 78 combat missions, earning three air medals for bravery and outstanding service
1952	Returns to Purdue University
1955	Graduates from Purdue University with Bachelor of Science degree in **Aeronautical Engineering**. Takes job at Lewis Flight Propulsion Laboratory and then taken as a **test pilot** at Edwards Air Force Base, California
1956	Marries Janet Shearon
1957	Son Eric is born
1959	Daughter Karen born (now deceased)

1962	Breaks altitude record (207,000 feet) in X–15 rocket plane. Accepted by **NASA** as an **astronaut**
1963	The Armstrongs' youngest child, Mark, is born
1965	Part of *Gemini 5* **backup crew**
1966	Commander of *Gemini 8* mission: brings capsule back to earth safely after docking problem with orbiting **satellite**
1968	Narrowly escapes death when **prototype** of **lunar module** crashes during training exercise
1968	Commands backup crew of *Apollo 8* mission, the first flight to go to the moon and back
1969	January 9: named as commander of *Apollo 11* mission to land on the moon July 20: becomes first human being to set foot on the Moon
1970-1	Acts as NASA chief of aeronautics activities
1971	Buys dairy farm near Lebanon, Ohio
1971-9	Serves as professor of aeronautical engineering at the University of Cincinnati
1986	Acts as vice-chairman of presidential commission investigating the *Challenger* space shuttle tragedy

"One leap for Mankind"—Neil Armstrong's first footprint on the surface of the moon

GLOSSARY

acrobatics performing dangerous or risky moves

active duty time spent fighting for one of the armed forces

aeronautical engineer someone who studies the science of flight

aircraft carrier ship on which planes can land and take off

altitude height off the earth's surface

anti-aircraft weapons that are designed to shoot down aircraft

astronaut a person who travels beyond the earth's atmosphere

astronomy the study of things outside earth's atmosphere

atmosphere the protective layer of oxygen, nitrogen and other gases that surrounds the earth

auditor someone who checks the way in which money is handled

aviation flying in human-made aircraft

backup crew team of astronauts who undergo the same training as the main crew in case they need to replace the main crew

biplane airplane with two sets of wings, one on top of the other

booby trap something that is hidden and intended to damage enemy fighters or machinery

cease-fire official agreement to end fighting

centrifuge long-armed device that swings around very quickly in order to produce force inside an object at the end of its arm

civilian someone who is not a member of any of the armed forces

cockpit the area of an aircraft or spacecraft where the pilots or astronauts operate control instruments

Cold War time lasting roughly from the end of the Second World War until the breakup of the Soviet Union (1991), when the United States and its western allies prepared for the possibility of war against the Soviet Union

command module part of an *Apollo* spacecraft that remained in **orbit** around the Moon

communist favoring the type of government of the former Soviet Union, in which the government owns nearly everything and individual freedom is limited

docking landing a craft in a specific area

dogfight battle between opposing military aircraft

ejection being propelled from a damaged aircraft to safety

Gemini stage of the U.S. space program that used spacecraft containing two astronauts

gravity force that causes objects to be attracted to each other

geologist person who studies rocks and their history

emigrate leave one country in order to settle in a different country

joint session rare meeting of both the U.S. House of Representatives and the U.S. Senate together in the same room

launch pad place from which a rocket is launched

lunar having to do with the Moon

Lunar Module part of an Apollo spacecraft that went to the Moon's surface and back again

Mercury stage of the U.S. space program that used spacecraft containing one astronaut

Mission Control the headquarters of the U.S. space program, in Houston, Texas

NASA National Aeronautic and Space Administration, which is responsible for the U.S. space flights

observatory place where a telescope is set up to study the sky

orbit travel in a route around an object, such as a satellite traveling around the Earth

propeller revolving blade which moves something forward

prototype early version of something, designed to test it before it is produced properly

ration control the sale of products in order to save money or vital material

reentry returning to the Earth through the atmosphere

satellite something that **orbits** a planet. It usually describes a human-made (or artificial) object

scholarship promise to pay for someone's education

Second World War a War (1939–1945) between Germany, Japan, and their supporters against Great Britain, the United States, the Soviet Union, and their supporters

simulate to create a situation similar to another one

Soviet Union powerful communist country that included Russia and many smaller nations, and which broke up in 1991

space race competition between the United States and the Soviet Union to reach certain milestones in space first

squadron group of two or more fighter planes that worktogether

test pilot someone who flies newly-designed aircraft in order to measure their overall speed, ability to move, and their general safety

thruster jet-propulsion rocket on a spacecraft

unemployed lacking a paying job and unable to earn a living

United Nations international group representing most of the world's countries

war effort extra work done to support a war

weightlessness sense of floating when people or objects are not subjected to gravity

western opposed to the general ideas of communist governments, and promoting open business practices and individual freedoms

wind tunnel channel in which a steady current of air can be blown in order to test the effect of wind on scale models of aircraft

INDEX

MORE BOOKS TO READ

Brown, Don. *One Giant Leap: The Story of Neil Armstrong.*
Boston, MA: Houghton, Mifflin Co. 1998.

Dunham, Montrew. *Neil Armstrong: Young Pilot.* NY: Simon
& Schuster. 1996.

Kramer, Barbara. *Neil Armstrong: The First Man on the Moon.*
Springfield, NJ: Enslow Publishers, Inc. 1997.